LEMURS!

A MY INCREDIBLE WORLD PICTURE BOOK

MY INCREDIBLE WORLD

Lemurs are native only to
the island of Madagascar,
off the coast of Africa.

1

Lemurs are **primates**, which means they are closely related to monkeys and apes.

There are over 100 different species of lemurs.

Lemurs can range in size from as small as a mouse to as large as a small dog!

Most species are active during the day (**diurnal**), although some are active at night (**nocturnal**).

Lemurs are **arboreal**, meaning they live in trees.

They have long, bushy tails
that they use for balance
when climbing.

Lemurs are social animals and usually live in groups called **troops**.

They communicate with each other using a variety of calls and body language.

Most lemurs are **herbivores**, meaning they eat only plants.

A few species are **omnivorous** and eat insects and small animals, as well.

Lemurs have a wet nose, which helps them smell their food and navigate their environment.

Their fingers and toes are long and slender, with sharp claws that help them cling to trees.

A female lemur is called a **princess**, while a male is called a **prince**.

Baby lemurs are called **pups**.

Female lemurs usually give birth to one or two babies at a time.

Pups are born with their eyes open and are able to climb and cling to their mother's fur almost immediately.

Lemurs have a unique tooth comb in their lower jaw that they use for grooming.

They have large, round eyes that
help them to see in low light.

Lemurs have excellent hearing and can detect high-frequency sounds.

Male lemurs engage in "stink fights," using their odor glands to assert dominance or mark territory!

Lemurs are incredible!

Printed in Great Britain
by Amazon

27591624R00016